FOREST ANIMALS
COLORING BOOK

DIANNE GASPAS

DOVER PUBLICATIONS, INC.
MINEOLA, NEW YORK

Planet Friendly Publishing
✔ Made in the United States
✔ Printed on Recycled Paper
Learn more at www.greenedition.org

At Dover Publications we're committed to producing books in an earth-friendly manner and to helping our customers make greener choices.

Manufacturing books in the United States ensures compliance with strict environmental laws and eliminates the need for international freight shipping, a major contributor to global air pollution.

And printing on recycled paper helps minimize our consumption of trees, water and fossil fuels. The text of *Forest Animals Coloring Book* was printed on paper made with 30% post-consumer waste, and the cover was printed on paper made with 10% post-consumer waste. According to Environmental Defense's Paper Calculator, by using this innovative paper instead of conventional papers, we achieved the following environmental benefits:

Trees Saved: 7 • Air Emissions Eliminated: 2,868 pounds
Water Saved: 3,610 gallons • Solid Waste Eliminated: 935 pounds

For more information on our environmental practices, please visit us online at www.doverpublications.com/green

Bibliographical Note

Forest Animals Coloring Book is a new work, first published by Dover Publications, Inc., in 2001.

DOVER *Pictorial Archive* SERIES

This book belongs to the Dover Pictorial Archive Series. You may use the designs and illustrations for graphics and crafts applications, free and without special permission, provided that you include no more than four in the same publication or project. (For permission for additional use, please write to Permissions Department, Dover Publications, Inc., 31 East 2nd Street, Mineola, N.Y. 11501.)

However, republication or reproduction of any illustration by any other graphic service, whether it be in a book or in any other design resource, is strictly prohibited.

International Standard Book Number

ISBN-13: 978-0-486-41316-7
ISBN-10: 0-486-41316-0

Manufactured in the United States of America
Dover Publications, Inc., 31 East 2nd Street, Mineola, N.Y. 11501

Introduction

The forests of eastern North America are renowned for their beauty during the autumn. Their brilliant yellow, orange, and red foliage draws visitors from around the world. But these forests are more than just a feast for the eyes. Each is a complex environment, supporting a variety of animal and plant life.

Many factors, including precipitation and temperature, determine what types of trees will grow in a particular area, and different climates produce different types of forests. The boreal forest, sometimes referred to as the northern coniferous forest, covers most of Canada and extends to the shores of Lake Superior, and, in places, into the Adirondack and Appalachian Mountains. Growing on land dotted with lakes and rivers formed by glaciers, this forest is made up primarily of spruce and fir in the north and pine and hemlock in the south. In the dense forest, little grows on the forest floor, but in areas where the forest is more open due to fire, or along the shores of lakes and rivers, wildflowers and other smaller plants flourish. In addition to many species of birds, insects, and smaller mammals, the boreal forest is home to large mammals such as the moose, bear, and wolf.

As you move into New England, New York, and the Allegheny Mountains of Pennsylvania, West Virginia, and Virginia, the evergreens are joined by deciduous trees to make up the transition forest. Here the trees are less dense and the undergrowth richer and more varied. With such a wide variety of plants available for food, an equally wide variety of animal life makes the transition forest its home. As you move south, more and more evergreens are replaced by deciduous trees to form the mixed deciduous forest.

Along the lower slopes of the Appalachian Mountains, north to New York and New England, west to the Ozarks of Arkansas and Missouri, and north to southern Michigan, is the oak-hickory forest, whose floor is covered with a undergrowth of shrubs and vines. South and east are the Southern Appalachians with over a hundred different species of trees, and still further south are the southern pinelands.

The boundaries between these and other types of forests are elastic and hard to determine, and no two forests are alike. But all provide a refuge for wildlife and an opportunity to observe and study many species that have been or could still be in danger of disappearing from our lives.

1. In the foreground, **honeybees** (*Apis mellifera*) gather nectar to produce honey. Common throughout the United States and lower Canada, honeybees live in hollow trees or in man-made hives. In the complex social structure within the hive, the queen bee mates with male drones and lays eggs. The sterile female workers gather nectar from flowers, produce the honey, and maintain the hive. Honeybees are reddish-brown to black with yellow stripes. The bright yellow **woodland sunflower** (*Helianthus strumosus*) blooms in August and September in woods, thickets, and clearings of transition, mixed deciduous, and oak-hickory forests. It is found from Quebec and New England to Georgia, west to Oklahoma and north to North Dakota.

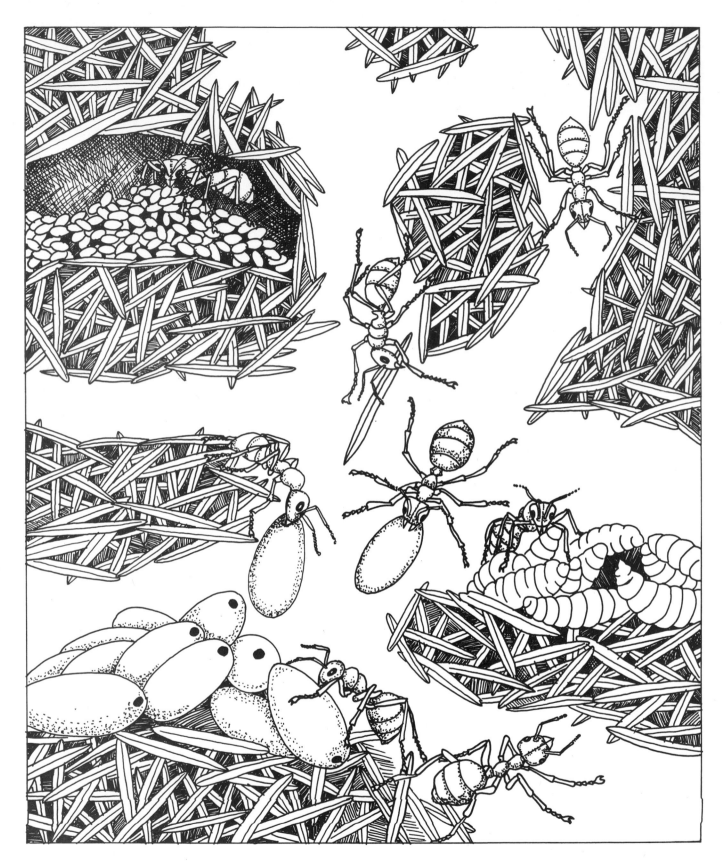

2. Here **black carpenter ant** (*Camponotus pennsylvanicus*) workers care for offspring in various stages of life. At the upper left are shown the eggs; directly below are cocoons containing pupae; to the right are larvae. These large (up to ½" long) brownish-black insects, found throughout the eastern United States, tunnel into the dead wood of trees, fallen logs, and other wood to build their nests and can do considerable damage to houses. Like bees, they have a hierarchial social structure centered around a queen, who is capable of laying thousands of eggs over her lifetime. Carpenter ants eat other insects, as well as fruit, sugar, and other sweets.

3. An **elephant stag beetle** (*Lucanus elephus*), also known as the **giant stag beetle**, is shown scurrying along a fallen log. This shiny reddish-brown insect has blackish antennae and legs; the male, shown here, has large horned antlerlike jaws. It is found in Virginia and North Carolina, and in mixed deciduous and oak-hickory forests as far west as Oklahoma and northeast to Illinois. Growing from the log are clusters of **golden mycena** (*Mycena leaiana*). These bright orange mushrooms are $\frac{1}{2}$" to 2" in diameter and $1\frac{1}{4}$" to $2\frac{3}{4}$" tall. They have salmon or orange-yellow gills with red-orange edges, orange to yellow stems, and white spores. They grow in the Southern Appalachians and in transition and mixed deciduous forests in the mid- to northeastern United States.

4. The pale green to brownish-gray coloring of the **Carolina mantid** (*Stagmomantis carolina*) enables it to blend in with vegetation. It eats caterpillars, moths, butterflies, flies, small wasps, bees, and bugs. It can be found in southern pinelands and in mixed deciduous forests from Virginia to Florida, **as far west as Mexico** and California, and northeast to Indiana. From August to October, the purplish stem of the **blue-stemmed goldenrod** (*Solidago caesia*) is covered with scattered clusters of tiny yellow flower heads. This common eastern flower can be found as far west as Texas and Wisconsin and from southern Ontario to Nova Scotia.

5. The **luna moth** (*Actias luna*), now considered an endangered species, is found only in broadleaf forests in the eastern half of the United States and southern Canada. This nocturnal moth is light green with light spots outlined in dark and has purple borders on the front of its forewings. It can have a wingspan of up to 3½". Here it rests on the silvery bark of the **yellow birch** (*Betula alleghaniensis*). The yellow birch, also known as **silver birch** and **gray birch**, is one of twelve birch representatives in North America. Growing 70 to 100 feet tall, it thrives in the Southern Appalachians and in transition forests in the northeast, the lake states, and in southern Canada. Its leaves are dark green on top and light yellow-green below, turning a brilliant yellow in the autumn.

6. The yellow-and-black **tiger swallowtail** (*Pterourus glaucus*) is one of most common butterflies of the eastern United States, with its range extending into central Alaska and Canada. Its hind wings have a row of blue patches merging with orange spots. The butterfly ranges in size from about 3" to 5½". One of the tallest of the eastern hardwoods, the 100- to 120-foot-tall **yellow-poplar** or **tuliptree** (*Liriodendron tulipifera*) has light gray bark, bright green leaves, and green-and-orange tuliplike flowers. The first branch is often as high as 60 feet above the ground. This beautiful tree grows in the Southern Appalachians, in southern pinelands, and in mixed deciduous forests in the eastern United States and southern Canada.

7. The brown-and-white **white-lipped forest snail** (*Triodopsis albolabris*) can move several inches a minute, leaving a trail of slime in its wake. It is found in wooded areas in the mid-Atlantic states and as far west as the Great Lakes, as well as in Texas and in some western states. As its name suggests, the tiny drab **acorn moth** (*Holcocera gladulella*) burrows inside acorns that have been abandoned by weevils. It is common in Pennsylvania, Ohio, and Indiana. The slow-moving brown **banded millepede** (*Narceus americanus*) can be found beneath rocks, wood, and leaves, or in soil in the mid- and southeastern United States. The dark brown **forest wolf spider** (*Lycosa gulosa*) in the foreground has grayish-yellow stripes. It hides among litter by day and hunts for small insects at night. Its range extends from Maine to Georgia, west to Utah, and north to southern Manitoba.

8. The high domed upper shell of the long-lived **Eastern box turtle** (*Terrapene carolina*) is black to brown with yellow, orange, or olive-green lines or spots. The front and rear sections of the lower shell are hinged and can be bent upward to completely close the edges of the shell. Although it sometimes cools off in ponds or puddles, this turtle is basically land-dwelling. It is found in damp forests, fields, and floodplains in the eastern half of the United States from southern Maine to the Florida keys and as far west as Texas in the south and Michigan and southern Illinois in the north. Here it is crawling over a fallen log of the **American beech** (*Fagus grandifolia*). This common eastern tree, 60 to 80 feet tall, has smooth, bluish-gray bark and leaves that are dark blue-green above, light green below. In the foreground are examples of the **destroying angel** (*Amanita virosa*), found in all forests throughout the United States and Canada. This poisonous white mushroom is 3" to 8" tall, with a 2"- to 5"- wide cap.

9. The nocturnal **American toad** (*Bufo americanus*), is commonly found in all forest types in the eastern half of the United States and Canada, although not in the extreme south. It can be green or brown or anywhere in between, patterned with lighter colors. It usually has one to two brown to orangish warts in each dark spot on its back. Its long tongue is attached at the front of its mouth and can be flipped out to catch insects—its major food. In the background is the dark blue-green **marginal shield fern** (*Dryopteris marginalis*),

growing 15" to 40" tall. The range of this eastern fern extends slightly into Canada. In the foreground is the colorful **two-colored bolete** (*Boletus bicolor*) found in the Southern Appalachians and in transition and mixed deciduous forests in the northeastern United States as far south as Georgia and as far west as Michigan. This mushroom has a purple-red cap with a bright yellow underside. The stem is yellow at the top and purple-red below. The spores are olive green.

10. The black to grayish-brown **five-lined skink** (*Eumeces fasciatus*) can be found in the damp woods of most forest types (except the boreal) in the eastern United States, from southern New England to Florida, west to Texas, Michigan, and Wisconsin, and into southern Canada. Adults have faded stripes and a gray tail; the coloration of the juvenile is much more brilliant. A breeding male has red-orange jaws. This lizard hibernates in the soil in winter. It eats insects, worms, spiders, lizards, crustaceans, and small mice. The **wood anemone** (*Anemone quinquefolia*) has starlike white ½"- to 1"-wide flowers that bloom from April to June. Its fluffy seeds are blown about and carried by the wind. It grows in the Southern Appalachians and in transition and mixed deciduous forests from Quebec to North Carolina.

11. The 2- to 6-foot-long **corn snake** (*Elaphe guttata*) has an arrow-shaped blotch on its head and red, gray, or brown spots ringed in black on a orange, tan, red, or gray background. This non-poisonous snake can be found in pine woods, and mixed deciduous, oak-hickory, and subtropical forests in the southeastern United States as far north as southern New Jersey. It can easily climb trees. The reddish-brown **white-footed mouse** (*Peromyscus leucopus*) is found in the Southern Appalachians and in transition, mixed deciduous, and oak-hickory forests in most of the eastern United States except the extreme southeast. It has a white belly and feet. It nests in old bird or squirrel nests, in stumps, buildings, logs, or below ground, and feeds on seeds, nuts, and insects, storing seeds and nuts for the future. In the left foreground is the **highland** or **highbush blueberry** (*Vaccinium corymbosum*), found in pine barrens, the Southern Appalachians, and transition and mixed deciduous forests in southeastern Canada and the United States as far south as Georgia. This shrub has smooth green leaves, with white to pink flowers and blue to blue-black berries.

12–13. The Boreal Forest. From left to right are: The **red-headed woodpecker** (*Melanerpes erythrocephalus*) is mostly black and white with large white wing patches, and has a red head and neck. It eats beechnuts, acorns, corn, fruits, insects, and the eggs and young of small birds. The **black spruce** (*Picea mariana*) grows 20 to 60 feet tall and has pale blue-green, four-sided needles with purple-brown cones near the top of the tree. Low branches sometimes take root when heavy snow causes them to bend to the ground, forming a ring of smaller trees around a large tree. **Moose** (*see plate* 42). **Eastern cottontail** (*see plate* 29). The **bunchberry** (*Cornus canadensis*) has tight greenish clusters of flowers and four white petal-like bracts. It has red,

berrylike clustered fruits. The powerful **wolverine** (*Gulo gulo*), found in northern Canada, has dark fur with broad yellowish bands on its forehead and sides. It eats mammals, fish, berries, and carcasses left by other predators. The **black-capped chickadee** (*Parus atricapillus*) is mostly light gray, with a black cap and throat and a white cheek patch. The wings are narrowly edged with white. This bird often feeds upside down. The **eastern chipmunk** (*Tamias stiatus*) spends most of its life on or below the ground, although it can climb trees. It is red-brown, with black-and-white stripes on its head, sides, and back. Its burrows are up to 12 feet long and include several chambers, along with several concealed entrances.

14. The **cedar waxwing** (*Bombycilla cedrorum*) spends the winter in the mixed deciduous forests of the lower half of the United States and the summer in the transition and boreal forests of the upper half of the United States and in Canada. This light brown bird has a black face mask, a pale yellow belly, a yellow-tipped gray tail, and red spots on its wings. Berries are a favorite food, but it also eats flower petals, sap, and insects. It is extremely sociable and travels in flocks. The **American mountain-ash** (*Sorbus americana*), found in the Southern Appalachians and in boreal and transition forests in the northeastern United States and southeastern Canada, grows 20 to 30 feet tall. It has white flowers and orange-red berries.

15. The nomadic **red crossbill** (*Loxia curvirostra*), found in boreal and transition forests in most of the United States (except the extreme south), and in southern and western Canada, follows the seed crops of conifers. It will nest any time of the year, even late in winter when food is plentiful. The plumage of the red crossbill varies greatly, but the male is typically brick red with dark wings and tail; the female is generally greenish-gray with dark wings and tail. The crossbill uses its beak to pry apart scales of cones while the tongue extracts the seeds. The 50- to 60-foot-tall **pitch pine** (*Pinus rigida*) is common in the eastern United States from southern Maine to northern Georgia. It has dark gray rough bark and 3"- to 5"-long yellow-green needles. The cones are broad at the base with rigid prickles. The pitch pine can grow on dry, rocky soil that will not support other trees.

16. The tiny (3" to 3½" long), metallic-green **ruby-throated hummingbird** (*Archilochus colubris*), found in all forest types, is the only hummingbird to breed east of Great Plains. The male's throat is metallic red; the female's dingy white. The hummingbird's long bill enables it to drink nectar from trumpet-shaped flowers without actually landing on the flower. It can hover and fly backwards and straight up and down. The **trumpet creeper** (*Campsis radicans*) climbs to 50 feet and has clusters of 2½"- to 3"-long orange to scarlet trumpet-shaped flowers. It blooms from July to September from New Jersey to Florida and west to Texas.

17. The **pileated woodpecker** (*Dryocopus pileatus*) is mostly black with white wing linings. Larger than other North American woodpeckers, it has a red crest and a striking black, white, and red striped pattern on its head. It is found in all forest types in the eastern United States, in Washington and Oregon, and in southern Canada. It makes its nest in trees infested with carpenter ants (a major food), first digging a large, usually rectangular, hole into the heart of the tree. The **white oak** (*Quercus alba*), 80 to 100 feet tall, can spread to 150 feet wide in open areas, with a trunk 3 to 4 feet in diameter. The bark is light gray, the leaves bright green above and pale below. Its range extends to southern Ontario and Quebec and from southern Maine to northern Florida, west to east Texas, and north to southeastern Minnesota.

18. The strikingly patterned **wood duck** (*Aix sponsa*) is commonly seen in forest lakes and ponds and in swamps and marshes in all forest types in the eastern half of the United States and into Canada, and also in the far west. The male, shown here, has a green head with a rust-red stripe below a white stripe, a white throat, rust-red chest, blue-black back and wings with lighter wing tips, a green tail, and a light brown lower body. The female is much less colorful and has a white teardrop-shaped eye patch. The wood duck feeds on various types of plant materials, including acorns. The female nests in trees, laying up to 15 eggs. The young ducks leave the nest soon after hatching.

19. The chunky **American woodcock** (*Philohela minor*) has rounded wings, short legs, a short tail, and a long bill. It is light brown with black crosswise bars on its head and white-and-dark-brown lengthwise stripes on its back. This protective "dead leaf" patterning makes it very hard to spot. The woodcock is nocturnal and rarely seen unless flushed, when its wings make a whistling sound as it takes flight. It lives in moist woodlands near clearings, alder thickets, and wet bottomlands in all forest types of the eastern half of the United States. The woodcock's primary food is earthworms, as well as insect larvae and occasional vegetable matter.

20. The **great horned owl** (*Bobo virginianus*) is found in all types of forests throughout most of the United States and Canada. This large owl is mottled brown or gray above and lighter below with fine dark barring, and has widely spaced ear tufts. It will attack any medium-sized mammal or bird and also eats beetles, lizards, and frogs. It usually lays its eggs in an old hawk or crow's nest, but sometimes in a hollow tree or cave. It has many varied calls, but the common call is a series of muffled hoots. A pair of mated horned owls in concert will seem to harmonize, with the female a third above the male.

21. One of the smallest of the North American birds of prey, the **sharp-shinned hawk** (*Accipiter striatus*) can be found in woodlands and brushy areas throughout the United States and Canada. It is gray above with black barring; its breast and the front part of the underwing are light brown striped with cinnamon. The female is larger than the male. This hawk preys on small mammals and birds such as the **American redstart** (*Setophaga ruticilla*). The male redstart is black with a white belly and orangish patches on its wings and tail; the female and immature birds are olive-brown above, white below with yellow patches. Its favored habitat is second-growth woodland, and it is found in most forest types in the eastern United States, the far west, and in southern Canada.

22. The nocturnal **silver-haired bat** (*Lasionycteris noctivagans*) has dark brown to black fur with white tips on its back, giving it a distinctive silvery appearance. This winged mammal is about 4" to 4½" long and has a 10" to 12½" wingspan. It can be found in the upper two thirds of the United States and the lower third of Canada. It flies in forests and roosts mainly in trees near water. Unlike most North American bats, who give birth to single young, this bat produces twins. Like all bats, the silver-haired bat can transmit rabies.

23. The **star-nosed mole** (*Condylura cristata*) lives most of its life underground and is active both day and night. It is a good swimmer and its tunnels often end in a pond or stream. This mole eats worms and insects, snails, crustaceans, even small fish. Its eyesight and sense of smell are poor, but its nose is surrounded by 22 fleshy, highly sensitive tentacles. It is generally dark brown or black with pinkish tentacles. It builds an underground spherical nest of grass or leaves and has one litter of 3–7 young per year, usually born between April to June. It can be found in moist, low-lying soil in the northeastern United States and eastern Canada.

24. The dark-metallic-gray **short-tailed shrew** (*Blarina brevicauda*) is one of the most common mammals in North America and is the only mammal in North America that has poisonous saliva. It feeds on insects and other invertebrates, and there is some evidence that it also eats small mice. Its head and body are 3" to 4" long; its tail is ¾" to 1". It lives in the Southern Appalachians and in transition and mixed deciduous forests in southeastern Canada and the northeastern United States. It makes its nest of dry leaves, grass, and hair beneath logs, stumps, rocks, or debris. The **margined burying beetle** (*Nicrophorus marginatus*), found in mixed deciduous forests throughout North America, hides during the day. This black carrion beetle has two interrupted yellow bands across its back. It feeds on dying and dead animals, and will drag a small carcass several feet before burying it beneath loose dirt.

25. Once prized by trappers, today the **American pine marten** (*Martes americana*) is found in boreal and transition forests in most of Canada, in northern New England and New York, around the Great Lakes, in the northern Rockies, and in the northwest. The marten spends much of its time in trees, but forages and moves on the ground. Its soft, dense fur varies from buff to dark brown on its back, shading to almost black on its legs and bushy tail. It has a pale gray head, a buff patch on its throat and breast, and pale brown underparts with irregular cream or orange spots. The marten eats chiefly squirrels and other small mammals, but also eats insects, birds, fruits, and nuts. The **eastern white pine** (*Pinus strobus*), 80 to 100 feet tall, grows in the northeastern United States and around the Great Lakes. Young trees have smooth, dark green bark; the bark of mature trees is dark brown and deeply cracked.

26. North American porcupine (*Erethizon dorsatum*) turns its back to its enemy, raises its long, stiff, barbed quills, and strikes out with its barbed tail. The quills are so loosely attached to the porcupine that they detach when they enter the attacker's skin. The grayish-brown nocturnal porcupine is most frequently seen in trees, although it is also a good swimmer. It can be found in boreal and transition forests in most of Canada, the northeastern United States, and around the Great Lakes, as well as west of the Rocky Mountains. The widespread **slippery elm** or **red elm** (*Ulmus rubra*) grows in transition, mixed deciduous, and oak-hickory forests in most of the eastern United States, except for the extreme northern and southern portions. It is 60 to 70 feet high and has red-brown bark.

27. The **beaver** (*Castor canadensis*) can be seen in all forest types in the eastern United States and Canada except the subtropical. North America's largest rodent is famed for its dam building ability. A mated pair of beavers first build an underwater foundation of mud and stone, then gnaw down trees and drag or float the cuttings to the dam site where they are incorporated into the foundation. In the pond formed behind the dam, they build a stick-and-mud lodge with underwater entrances. This lodge is occupied by family groups of parents, yearlings, and kits. The beaver is rich brown with a naked, scaly, black tail. Its preferred food is aspen, poplar, birch, maple, willow, and alder. In late summer and fall, it stores wood cuttings in an underwater food pile to be eaten in winter. The kits are born in spring and stay in the home pond until they are about two years old.

28. The **long-tailed weasel** (*Mustela frenata*) changes color dramatically, from brown in the spring and summer to yellowish-white in the winter. Although temperature does play a role, this change is triggered mainly by changes in the length of the day and takes place over about four weeks. The tip of its tail is black.

The mostly nocturnal weasel eats squirrels, chipmunks, birds, rats, and mice. It is usually found near water and lives in western Canada and in most of the United States in transition, mixed deciduous, and oak-hickory forests, and in pine barrens and southern pinelands.

29. The **eastern cottontail** (*Sylvilagus floridanus*) is found east of the Rockies in all forests except the boreal. The most common rabbit in North America, the eastern cottontail produces several litters per year, and rabbits born in early spring may breed that summer. The cottontail feeds on green vegetation in summer, barks and twigs in winter. It is brownish or grayish in color with a white tail and a rusty patch on the nape of its neck. The **shagbark hickory** (*Carya ovata*), 70 to 80 feet tall, grows in the Southern Appalachians, in pine barrens, and in mixed deciduous and oak-hickory forests in the eastern United States. Its light gray bark hangs in long loose strips curving away from the trunk.

30. The nocturnal **raccoon** (*Procyon lotor*) lives in all forest types throughout most of the United States and into southern Canada. It is gray to black, and has a black face mask and a bushy tail with alternating rings of black and yellowish-white. Raccoons feed mostly along streams and lakes, eating fruits, nuts, grains, insects, frogs, crayfish, and birds' eggs. In captivity, it will dunk its food in water before eating, giving rise to the belief that it "washes" its food. This is not a sign of cleanliness, but believed to reflect the fact that its natural habit is to find food in water. The raccoon usually makes its dens in hollow trees with an entrance at least 2½ feet above the ground, but will also make a den in hollow logs, rock crevices, ground burrows, or human buildings.

31. The **eastern gray squirrel** (*Sciurus carolinensis*) lives in the eastern United States in all forest types except the boreal, and is rarely found away from trees. It nests in holes in trees or builds a leaf nest in branches. This brownish-gray squirrel has a bushy gray tail bordered with white-tipped hairs. It eats berries, nuts, fungi, and fruits, and acts as a reforestation agent by storing nuts and acorns singly in small holes in the ground; many of these are never recovered and grow to become trees. It is active all year long and generally has two litters of 3–5 young per year.

32–33. The Oak-Hickory Forest. From left to right: The **bur** or **mossy cup oak** (*Quercus macrocarpa*) grows 70 to 80 feet tall. The blue-gray **white-breasted nuthatch** (*Sitta carolinensis*) climbs down tree trunks head first to gather insects and their eggs from the bark. The **shining sumac** (*Rhus copallina*), about 25 feet tall, has light brown or gray bark and shiny dark green leaves that turn dark reddish-purple in the fall. **Fowler's toad** (*Bufo woodhousei fowleri*) is yellow, green, or brown, with a light line down the middle of its back. The **blue jay** (*Cyanocitta cristata*) is bright blue above with black barring, and white on its wings and tail. It eats seeds, insects, fruit, nuts, smaller birds, mice, frogs, snails, and small fish. **White-tailed deer** (*see plate 40*). **Eastern**

gray squirrel (*see plate 31*). The male **northern cardinal** (*Cardinalis cardinalis*) is a bright red, the female brownish-yellow with red on the wings and tail. It has a varied musical repertoire, and the male and female may sing alternately. **Long-tailed weasel** (*see plate 28*). The **pignut hickory** (*Carya glabra*), 60 to 80 feet tall, has light gray bark, light green leaves that turn yellow in the fall, and dark brown rounded or pear-shaped fruit. The **buttonbush** (*Cephalanthus occidentalis*) has dark green oval leaves, white fragrant flowers in clusters, and round red-brown fruit.

34. The nocturnal **spotted skunk** (*Spilogale putorius*) is black with white spots on its head, broken white stripes on its body, and has a bushy tail with a white tip. It can be found in the southern and mid-eastern United States as far north as Pennsylvania, and in the midwest. When attacked it raises its hindquarters and sprays its foe with an unpleasant smelling musk. It eats mice, rats, and other small animals in the winter, adding insects to its diet in the spring and summer. The **eastern screech owl** (*Otus asio*), found in the eastern two-thirds of the United States, can be reddish, brown, or gray. Both of these animals can be found in all eastern forest types except the boreal. In the left foreground is the green or purplish-brown **jack-in-the-pulpit** (*Arisaema triphyllum*), which blooms from April to July in mixed deciduous and oak-hickory forests in the eastern two-thirds of the United States and Canada, in the Southern Appalachians, and in the southern pinelands.

35. The nocturnal **southern flying squirrel** (*Glaucomys volans*) can glide up to 80 yards from the top of trees, using the loose folds of skin between its front and back legs as "sails." It moves its legs to control the glide, and its tail acts as a rudder. One of the smallest tree squirrels, the southern flying squirrel is grayish-brown above and white below. It can be found in broad-leaved and mixed forests in the eastern half of the United States, except northern New England and the tip of Florida. The **eastern hemlock** (*Tsuga canadensis*), found in the Southern Appalachians and in transition and mixed deciduous forests in the northeastern United States and southeastern Canada, is a long-lived, slow developing tree, growing 60 to 70 feet tall. It has cinnamon-brown bark, flat needles that are shiny dark green on top, whitish below, and small cones on the tips of its branches.

36. The nocturnal **Virginia opossum** (*Didelphis virginiana*), found in most types of forests except the boreal throughout the eastern United States, is whitish-gray to nearly black, with a white face and black ears. It often hangs upside down by its tail, and, when cornered, may feign death. Young opossums remain in the mother's pouch for about 2 months, then may travel on her back, wrapping their tails around hers to stay in place. The **flowering dogwood** (*Cornus florida*), 20 to 30 feet tall, has flowers with four white petal-like bracts and red berrylike fruit. It is found in most forest types except the boreal in southeastern Canada, and in the eastern United States from Maine to north Florida, and west to Texas. The **sulphur polypore** (*Polyporus sulphureus*) grows in large clusters on trunks, logs, and stumps of conifers and broad-leaved trees in most forest types. It is 2" to 20" wide with a short or absent stem, and has a orange, salmon, or yellow cap with a ruffled edge, and a sulphur-yellow underside.

37. The **red fox** (*Vulpes vulpes*) found in most of the United States and Canada in all types of forests, usually, but not always, has a reddish face and back and white underparts. It can also be black, black with silver-tipped hairs, reddish-brown with a cross across the shoulders, and other colorations, but it always has a white-tipped bushy tail. The fox eats small mammals and birds as well as insects, fruit, and carrion. It usually makes its den in porous soil on a slope and often keeps a spare den to move into in case of danger. The red fox has one litter per year, born in the spring. The pups remain in the den for about a month, then come out to play. In the right foreground are a group of **bluets** (*Houstonia caerulea*), sometimes called **Quaker ladies**. These pale blue flowers with golden-yellow centers bloom from April to June in the Southern Appalachians and in transition, mixed deciduous, and oak-hickory forests from Ontario to Georgia and west to Alabama and Wisconsin.

38. The **wild boar** (*Sus scrofa*) and the **domestic pig** are the same species. Although some European boars have been reintroduced in this country, most American wild boar are feral domestic pigs. Their diet includes roots, tubers, bulbs, fungi, green vegetation, grains, nuts, invertebrates, small vertebrates, and carrion. Most wild boar have dark gray, black, or brown stiff bristles; the piglets are striped. The basic family unit is a female and her piglets; males are solitary unless mating. At the lower right is **devil's bit** (*Chamaelirium luteum*), also called **fairy wand** and **blazing star**. The clusters of tiny flowers are white. It grows in transition and mixed deciduous forests in southern Ontario and in the eastern United States as far south as Florida. In the background is the 50- to 60-foot-high conical **red spruce** (*Picea rubens*), found in transition forests in southeastern Canada and the eastern United States as far south as North Carolina, and in the Southern Appalachians.

39. The **gray wolf** (*Canis lupus*), is now found primarily in the boreal forests of Canada and Alaska, although it has been reintroduced into the United States in recent years. Although usually gray, it can vary from nearly white to black. The wolf mates for life, and has a complex social organization and a rigid hierarchy. The pack, normally four to seven wolves, is ruled by a dominent (alpha) male. The pack will hunt big game, primarily deer and caribou. When big game is scarce, wolves will feed on anything. The **paper birch** (*Betula papyrifera*) (the thinner tree in the drawing), has chalky white bark, peeling in thin strips. It grows 50 to 70 feet tall. The **jack pine** (*Pinus banksiana*) grows 30 to 70 feet tall and has scaly brown bark. Both are found in boreal and transition forests in Canada and the northern United States.

40. The **white-tailed deer** (*Odocoileus virginianus*), found in all forest types throughout the United States and lower Canada, is the one of the most abundant wild hoofed mammals in North America. It stands about three feet tall at the shoulder and has a grayish-brown coat in the winter and a tan or reddish-brown coat in the summer. When alarmed, it raises its tail, showing the white underside. Male deer begin growing their antlers several months after birth and shed them each winter. The white-tailed deer browses on twigs, shrubs, fungi, acorns, grass, and herbs. It is most often seen in the early morning and or at dusk.

41. The **black bear** (*Ursus americanus*), is widely distributed in the boreal forests of Canada, and in transition forests in the United States as far south as Florida. Adults are 4½ to 6 feet long, stand 2 to 3 feet high at the shoulder, and weigh between 200 to over 475 pounds. The cubs are very small relative to their adult size. Black bears have a brown snout, and a small white breast spot is often present. They feed on animals ranging from insects to large mammals, as well as on plant material, carrion, and garbage. The 50- to 80-foot-tall **red pine** or **Norway pine** (*Pinus resinosa*) can be found in transition forests in southern Canada, New England, around the Great Lakes, and along the Atlantic seaboard as far south as Pennsylvania. It has red-brown bark and 4"- to 6"-long needles bunched near the branch tips.

42. The largest member of the deer family, the **moose** (*Alces alces*) can weigh more than 1000 pounds. It is 7 to 10 feet long and stands 5 to 6½ feet high at the shoulder. Once nearly vanished from the United States, it can now be seen in the boreal forests of New England, the Great Lakes area, the northern Rockies, and Canada. It has a dark brown or reddish-brown coat with lighter legs and underparts. Males shed their massive, flattened, pronged antlers in the winter and grow them anew in spring. During the fall mating season, the males become restless and aggressive, and will fight one another. Calves (often twins) are born in the spring, and remain hidden and inactive for several days. Moose eat many kinds of vegetation including aquatic plants in the summer; woody plants, twigs, bark, and saplings in winter.

43. The **bobcat** (*Felis rufus*), the most common wild feline in North America, is widely distributed in the United States and southern Canada, occurring in a wide variety of forests—transition, mixed deciduous, subtropical, the Southern Appalachians, and southern pinelands—as well as in other habitats. It has tawny fur and a spotted belly. Its tail is black on top, buff to brown below. It is nocturnal, essentially solitary, and very territorial. It will eat almost any mammal, reptile, or bird, although rabbits and hares are its usual food. The bobcat makes its den in caves, hollow logs, or on rocky ledges. As shown here, it is a good climber. The **red maple** or **swamp maple** (*Acer rubrum*) grows 60 to 90 feet tall in all forest types in the eastern United States and southern Canada. Its leaves are light green above, gray-green below and turn bright red in fall.

Index of Common Names

Index of Scientific Names